LIFE
Learning Instructions For Everyone
... in prison and out

LIFE
Learning Instructions For Everyone
... in prison and out

Phillip Vance Smith, II

Cover Design by Casey Chiappetta and Lewis Whitmire
Text Design by Charlotte Lopez-Jauffret
Text Editing by Kat Bodrie

BleakHouse Publishing
2024

BleakHouse Publishing

Kerwin Building 254
American University
Washington, D.C. 20016

www.BleakHousePublishing.org

Robert Johnson – Publisher
Norah Nasser – Chief Operating Officer
Ginger Finigan – Chief Editorial Officer
Kat Bodrie – Book Editor
Ben Feder – Art Director

Copyright © 2024 by Phillip Vance Smith, II

All rights reserved. No part of this book shall be reproduced or transmitted in any form or by any means, electronic, mechanical, magnetic, photographic including photocopying, recording or by any information storage and retrieval system, without prior written permission of the publisher. No patent liability is assumed with respect to the use of the information contained herein. Although every precaution has been taken in the preparation of this book, the publisher and author assume no responsibility for errors or omissions. Neither is any liability assumed for damages resulting from the use of the information contained herein.

ISBN: 978-0-9961162-9-9

Printed in the United States of America

For those who never give up . . . keep fighting.

Table of Contents

Acknowledgements
Author's Note
Editor's Note

Lesson 1: Life
"what is prison really like?" – 3
lifer – 5
old coon – 7
what's in a name? – 9
count – 11
kaleidoscope of the condemned – 13
the picture man – 15
new friends – 18

rich – 21

Lesson 2: Love
why? – 29
lipstick on a toad – 30
you and me – 31
fifteen minutes – 32
mr. maytag – 33
i, sorrow – 35
ceaseless change – 36

the inheritance – 39

Lesson 3: Hurt & Tragedy
just over the fence – 45
life is death – 46
suicide prevention – 47
children of the chain – 48
the satirical comedy of life – 49
gunslinger – 54
ode to oroonoko – 60

an insufficient apology – 63

mammaw – 71

Lesson 4: Injustice
no coal burning – 79
appropriate violence – 81
raising cain – 82
banned books – 86
a moral dilemma – 88
hopeless hustle – 92
ho-ass nigga – 96
i remain – 98

grandad – 101

Lesson 5: Redemption
at the well – 107
recollection – 110
hope – 111
Learning Instructions For Everyone – 112
time – 113
the introvert – 114
"what could prison be?" – 116

About the Poet
About the Artists, Editors, & Designers
Praise for *LIFE*
Review of *LIFE*
Other Titles from BleakHouse Publishing

Acknowledgements

Gratitude goes to the editors of the publications in which some of these poems originally appeared:

Beneath Our Numbers – "the inheritance"

Cage – "why?," "lipstick on a toad," "you and me," "children of the chain"

Tacenda Literary Magazine – "lifer"

Walk In Those Shoes – "the inheritance," "'what is prison really like?'"

Author's Note

As a self-taught poet, I am unburdened by a particular style. I admire many poets, like Emily Dickinson, Langston Hughes, and especially Charles Bukowski, but I do not care to mimic their style. Freethinking allows me to create as an individual divorced from the rules, structure, or poetic dogma pioneered by someone else.

The only consistent feature of my work is the usage of the inclusio: a literary mechanism that places the title of a piece at the beginning and the end. I don't know why I began using it. I didn't know the term "inclusio" existed until I learned it in college. By then, I had employed it in my poems for well over a decade. I continue using the inclusio because it adds a unique quality to my work, and it feels natural. When I look over an old poem, I often ponder the title at the end, thinking about what I just read and how the concluding title reaffirms the intention of the piece.

I began writing poetry as therapy — to expel frustrations I felt as a youth serving life without parole in a violent, uncaring environment. Those early poems reflected the violence and misogyny promoted in the hip hop songs I loved. Maturity taught me that vulnerability was much more useful to me than the false bravado I emulated. This realization helped me write with honesty.

Any personal proceeds for this book have been donated to OurJourney (ourjourney2gether.com), a reentry nonprofit started by formerly incarcerated people. I will not take a dime, because I wrote this book to share what I've learned about life, love, hurt, tragedy, injustice, and redemption.

This collection compiles poetic images from my personal experiences and fictional storytelling ability. Because I have spent over twenty years in prison, my words will not always evoke the image of a rose or the scent of jasmine. I write in the moment — about whatever the moment creates — and I write unapologetically about prison.

One piece, for instance, "gunslinger," illustrates how some incarcerated men expose themselves to female correctional staff. It is graphic. It can be difficult to read, even for me. But I write about these things to explain why they happen and how we are all traumatized by their occurrence.

Ignoring the traumatic events we witness only adds more trauma to our lives, because ignoring something prevents recognizing how it hurts us. If I know about anything, it is pain. To become free from pain, we must confront it, no matter how hurtful. Only recognition of pain can lead to freedom from it. My poetry recognizes much of the pain I caused and pain caused to me.

In this collection, you will find fiction like "ode to oroonoko" and "a hopeless hustle," which amplify awareness to injustice. Other pieces, like "rich" or "i, sorrow," are memoirs that preserve my memory of a life experience.

I never expected to become a published poet. My words were meant to reflect, to remember, and to reveal my innermost feelings to myself. I am honored that my editor Kat Bodrie saw promise in my work and recommended publication with BleakHouse. Enjoy.

> Phillip Vance Smith, II
> February 6, 2023

Editor's Note

I reached out to Phill after reading a blog post he'd written for Emancipate NC. The North Carolina prison mailing system had recently switched from mail sent directly to prisons to a scan-send-and-print company called TextBehind, which has a P.O. Box out of Maryland.

Phill wrote about losing long-term friends due to this change. Some were afraid of the fact that their letters would now be digitally stored for seven years, their privacy snatched by anyone with access. Some refused to fund TextBehind by not sending letters through their convenient smartphone app. (Read Phill's investigative piece about TextBehind at logicmag.io/supa-dupa-skies/lost-in-transit-digitization.)

As someone who navigated the switchover, I decided to write Phill a "helpful" letter, introducing myself and giving unsolicited advice. Sure enough, Phill didn't need my help, but I learned some things about him that connected us in other ways. I'd heard from a friend on death row about legislation that could give people with life without possibility of parole (LWOP) sentences a second chance through stringent educational, behavioral, and vocational programming. Turns out, Phill was a co-author of the bill, The Prison Resources Repurposing Act, which was introduced in the 2021 NC House session and re-introduced in 2023.

Not only that: Phill is also a creative writer. His book *Cage*, sold on Amazon under the pseudonym Vance Phillips, artfully combines prose and poetry and follows a fictional prisoner through his day-to-day life working in the prison's warehouse and writing love poetry about a particular guard in his spare time. I was intrigued by how Phill reveals the nuances of the prison's social ecosystem and how his main character breaks through the common stereotype of prisoners, a character trait I figured Phill shared as well.

You'll find a few of the poems from *Cage* in this book. These are earlier works that speak to the difficulties of sustaining love when one partner has a life sentence — which, for LWOP, is basically a death sentence.

Phill began writing other poems about the prison experience, and I immediately pitched Phill's poetry to Robert Johnson, BleakHouse's publisher, with whom I'd worked on George T. Wilkerson's books in 2022. Phill's style is markedly different from George's: less narrative, more rhyming. Many of Phill's lines are melodic and verge on spoken word — so much so that we asked Phill to read a few poems for us. You can find recordings of them on the BleakHouse website, bleakhousepublishing.org, or scan the QR code at the end of this book.

At first, I didn't know what to think about Phill's technique of putting a poem's title at the beginning *and* at the end of the poem. It did help, as I often go back to the title after I finish reading the poem, scavenging for more meaning. Phill taught me that this technique is called an inclusio, and he has his own reasons for using it. I love when he seamlessly flows from the body of the poem into the title at the end, making it one grammatically cohesive unit. The poem has its own magic then.

I guess editors talk about finding certain poets "promising," and this is what I knew about Phill: he was full of potential. He wrote most of these poems in the span of a few months in 2022. It's clear how much his craft has developed since the days of *Cage*, and many of the new topics are searing commentary about life sentences and the criminal justice system. I share many of his views, and although only one section of the book is titled "Hurt & Tragedy," you'll find these themes scattered throughout.

Prison is full of tragedy and pain, suffering and heartache. It's amazing that people like Phill can live in this environment and not only survive, but flourish. I think part of it has to do with the power of writing to transform us when we simply put into words our thoughts and feelings, which prisoners usually suppress in favor of appearing "strong."

But true strength comes from vulnerability, and Phill is a brave individual (and Renaissance man) who puts himself out there — and we are all the more blessed and better for it.

    Kat Bodrie
    March 9, 2023

Lesson 1: Life

"what is prison really like?"

"what is prison really like?"
she asks . . . so i muse . . .

it is stale breath
in chow lines
crammed behind vikings who
haven't showered in months

or . . . racial divides
like lawmakers
fistfights over what to watch
street outlaws vs love & hip hop
MAGA vs #BLM
acronyms of the violence
we kill to view
acronyms of the society
we thought we once knew

in this zoo
hallways twist in a maze
leading past a monkey's cage
fronted by plexiglas that displays
        thieves = chimps
        rapists = orangutans
        killers = gorillas
broken men who fall here
only to be broken again
in a pool of blood
from a shank's puncture wound
seeping out like the hope
left in courtrooms

yet . . . it can be an awakening
of the spirit and soul
to encounter dickinson, hughes,

angelou, emerson, and bukowski
then to mimic them in my own
gravelly voice
rubbed hoarse by decades of
silent activism
in my cell
with a pen as a shovel
digging me out of
this hell

while staring at her face
across the visitation table
i repeat her question
but more as a question
to myself

i muse ... before asking ...
"what is prison really like?"

lifer

lifer
the correctional officer says
good morning
i ask
what's so good about it
she replies
you're alive
humph
why is life such a good thing

they say
waking up
is a gift
but they've never
been awakened
to the sound
of men screaming
as homemade knives
pierce bellies and necks
because they used
the bloods' phone
or didn't pay the crips rent
or called an aryan brother
a bitch
before breakfast

they say
waking up
is a gift
but they've never
been awakened
three times
during the night
for headcounts
with a flashlight
beaming in their eyes

to verify
that their sorry ass
is still
alive

they say
life is a precious gift
i ask
a gift of what
living in prison
waiting to die
because that's
the only way
i'll see the outside

they say
life is a gift
humph
prison
makes me wish
someone would
take it back
lifer

old coon

old coon
dallas and i were sitting on the yard
watching a game of block basketball.
he pointed to the youngest man on the court.
we called him noody.
he had no facial hair.
skin softer than the underbelly of a newborn seal.
"that was you, when you came in, luck," dallas said.
he would know.
dallas was pushing fifty when i came in
at twenty-three.
we called grizzled, gray-haired cons like him old coons,
no matter their race.
like grumpy grandpas
they frowned upon boisterous conversation,
cutting silence like sirens signaling disaster.
when josh slit jack's throat for calling
him a son-of-a-bitch in the chow line,
the old coons in my block locked in.
"don't never get in folks' business," they said later.
they called me young buck, youngblood, or young man.
i used to mistake solitude for weakness, until
i saw a sixty-three-year-old man stab a young
guy so hard that i could hear the shank's point
hitting concrete with each thrust.
i learned to respect a man's space then.
a man twice my age taught me to
make a shank.
he gave me a bottle of oil to grease my
concrete floor so i could slick the groove.
i scraped the metal rod through, thousands of
times a night.
he also taught me good sense.
i never used that shank, and never needed another.
as my beard filled in, my hairline receded.
years of concrete and steel brittled my bones.

jokes that once made me laugh stopped being funny.
my black hair turned to gray.
i understood why old coons frowned at loud noise.
when the basketball game ended,
noody ran over and pointed to his water bottle beside me.
"yo, unc. let me get that bottle."
i stared at noody dripping sweat,
and i could no longer remember what it felt like
to be so young.
i looked to dallas,
but for some reason, he hadn't aged a bit.
old coon

Note: The phrase "old coon" refers to a dated racial slur once used to describe a wise, black older convict. Now the term is used to describe older cons of all races.

what's in a name?

what's in a name?
i entered yellow pod on the sixth
floor of the wake county jail for
the first time at age twenty. huge
detainees stretching faded, orange
jumpsuits demanded my name. i didn't
know what to say. i was from pasty-white
suburbia, not black rough raleigh, so no
one had ever seen me slinging dope in the
'hood. that house of concrete and steel wouldn't
respect phillip vance smith, the second — more
title than name.
so i created . . . a new me . . .

in the past two decades, i've encountered many names.
some made sense, others were just plain strange.
handles are as common as bars in prison,
but as a youth, some names proved hard to envision . . .
    like . . .

frog, gator, showtime, rasta mack,
skeeter, snapper, cool, and cadillac black.

dice, jet, fu, big show,
zulu, wise, cipher, and c-lo

some monikers originated from way back
like a grandma's nickname for my man popjack.
handles make government names fade like a vestige
as some prefer sending a sinister message . . . like . . .

blood raw, savage, killa, homicide,
crazy, snake, blade, and tech nine.

osama, made man, tank, smoke,
stove pipe, razor, soldier, and rope.

nicknames indicate a reflection of self,
like associating rothschild with prestige and wealth.
sometimes, negative names get stuck
but i'll never regret naming myself "badluck."
what's in a name?

count

count
"everybody up!
count time! count time! count time!"

an officer walks the dorm, jiggling cell doors
making sure we're locked in, like valuables in a store
if i'm sleeping, they knock, just to see me move
the most sleep i ever get is only an hour or two

"count time! count time! count time!"

five times daily, they count us as cattle
on a plantation of pain, reminiscent of chattel
at times, a count can last up to an hour
once, it took three, when walt died near the shower
they rolled him out stiff, his life/hope drained
i wondered if he ever worried about dying in a cage

"count time! count time! count time!"

i used to loathe count time; i hated being alone
isolated with problems for which i never atoned
instead of getting high or wasting away the day
i had to confront my past and my future gone astray

"count time! count time! count time!"

i got used to the count after years in a cell
if i have to be locked in, it doesn't have to be hell
sometimes i meditate, sometimes i write
sometimes i count my accomplishments in life

"count time! count time! count time!"

i found a melody in stillness, one i'll try to describe
it's a tempo of silence with de-crescendoing sighs

when the prison settles down and shouts of ignorance cease
my spirit eases slowly into a cadence of peace
count

kaleidoscope of the condemned

kaleidoscope of the condemned
press an eye to the glass and see what i have seen
in psychedelic confetti scattered inside me

walls and fences topped with sharpened razor wire
batteries and staples to macgyver caveman's fire

my man b.i. in my cell, helping bag up trees
forced into selling weed to buy soap from the canteen

letter from the court, my lawyer blew the appeal
punching brick walls to mimic the pain i feel

begging a counselor to give me a better job
because forty cents a day only compels men to rob

tattoos on faces depict a gangland mosaic
these lawless cages create a predator's oasis

some penitentiary preacher peddling stories about jesus
i'd rather study law to secure early releases

blood on the walls stole my religion
but paranoid schizos sharpen my vision

"you penitentiary preachers peddling stories about jesus!
if god exists, then goddamn, why don't he teach us?"

a madman screams, who's in need of medication
it's three a.m., he's fucking trying my patience

staring at my mother who has given up hope
through dirty glass in visitation, she's impossible to console

a letter from my lady says she needs to move on
i didn't expect her to stick around for this damn long

c/o's tear up cells worse than the gestapo
terrorizing us like cow pokes from el dorado

hating myself for masquerading as a thug
questioning why black boys must appear tough

razor blade, like a sword, clenched in my fist
but no courage to commit seppuku to my wrists

press your eye to the glass to see what i see
this confetti of lunacy that will never escape me
kaleidoscope of the condemned

the picture man

the picture man
my job is simple.
enter visitation;
pull the camera out of the cabinet;
collect his two-dollar picture ticket;
get his family in front of a seasonal mural;
snap however many pics he bought;
print the pictures.

a muslim once explained that allah
doesn't allow picture taking because
photos trap the soul. as an atheist,
i thought he was crazy. becoming the
picture man taught me different.

the camera captures smiles of those
who haven't had reason to smile
in a long while. a child clutches
his father's leg for the one-hundred-twenty
minutes they share, anticipating the one-hundred-twenty
years they must be apart. the mother smiles,
but not really a smile. her joy, temporary and
destroyed by loneliness. she smiles to preserve
an image of togetherness she does not feel.

"ready for your picture?" i ask a
couple — pen pals — meeting for
the first time. they pose miles
apart. her afraid to touch. him
afraid to test the bond built by
the anonymity of letters.
"squeeze in," i say. "i ain't got all day."
inane rules ricochet in my head:
hands above waist. no shots
with his crotch against her buttocks,
no kissing, no fondling — makes for an

awkward photo — but somehow,
i coach them closer to love.

a boy bolts in dressed for
little league. baby sister follows, a smiling
jack-o-lantern. then a teen,
once in cap and gown, returns this
week in fatigues, just before
deploying to the middle east. they enter
like costumed treats for halloween, but life
plays a trick when they must leave. they
arrive week after week, spending no more
time with dad than they spend with me.

the visiting room is circled
by windows. natural light waterfalls
in, sending families roaring down rapids
of memory lane, illuminating the
worst men
at their best.

tuesday through saturday. three
visits each. when i leave,
a male officer escorts me
out. i hand him one item at
a time. shirt. pants. sock. sock.
boxers. "squat. cough. lift up
your nuts. spread your butt." i
walk through a metal detector
naked. i dress, immune to the
inhumane. oblivious to the
obvious despite the constant
destruction of my dignity, i smile,
remembering the prisoner down on one
knee. his proposal surprised her as much
as it did me.
i raised the camera.
snap. snap. snap.

the flash
froze tears in icicles to
commemorate her
happy day
but after two hours, she too
left, leaving us alone, but
with a memento
of her love
in an image of
her trapped soul from
the picture man

new friends

new friends
i see them, sitting happily at a table
laughing while swapping war stories and fables

the same ol' yarn, about loving some girl
burglarizing her house; pawning grandmama's pearls

lies he's told a million times
varied laugh cues and rhythm, but a familiar rhyme

later... they huddle over stacks of pictures
his daughter plays soccer; his son is a pitcher

this fresh friendship could last for all ages
until the new arrival finds out...
this guy's a statutory rapist
new friends

rich

rich
our house,
a lemon three-story with
a wrap-around porch was
the nicest, drawing our
neighbor's awe, envy, and
scorn.
i was the
only
black kid
for miles.
an ant traversing
an oceanic bleached
bedsheet called
the south.

one sunny day,
a ginger from the
trailer park up the street
had skipped class to fish
in our lake.
when i got off the school
bus, he yelled, "rich nigger!
rich nigger!" as if success
deserved disrespect.

his jealousy stabbed my
soul, implying a
disconnect to what
a nigger was supposed
to be.

my mother had fled her chicago
ghetto for atlanta with
two hungry kids and

only fifty dollars in her
pocket.

i wore blue jeans until mouths
gaped at the knees,
screaming poverty.
she ironed on mismatched
denim patches to
silence them.

but i never went naked.

we ate grits for dinner when
we couldn't afford rice, like slaves
sopping with their fingertips.

but i never went hungry.

she worked two jobs,
saved, scraped, and
scrimped.
she went days without
talking as the
stress
ate her alive.
not only
did she fight
to survive,
she fought a double
jeopardy:
born both black and female.

my mother was not gifted
an inheritance or
given success. she
did not stumble upon it
like a techie with an idea.
she earned it.

but the unsuccessful cannot

understand that our expensive
house wasn't much different
than their trailer.
everyone works for what they
want. bigger checks = bigger bills.
it just looked nicer
from the outside.

when i told her what
the white boy
shouted while fishing
in our lake,
she sighed and said
something like,
if he
really knew us,
he'd know that
we
have
never
been
rich

Phillip's mother, Allean Finley, around 1979, listening to
Phillip's father's band play at a club in Chicago

Lesson 2: Love

why?

why?
why would she want me?
i have nothing — i offer even less.
i possess not the confidence most men profess.
why would she want me?
i have no aspiration, no dreams to fulfill,
no fast-talking words to make her feet stand still.
my emotions are fragile; self-esteem has been killed.
why would she want me?
brutal truths are too truthful; their honesty i know.
yet i find myself basking in her radiant glow.
golden lamp lighting darkness — she spotlights my show.
her pleasure — center stage — but i script sorrow.
why would she want me?
my heart . . . so dark as a raven on a wire.
so craven as a coward cowering beneath sire.
when fanning the flames of my sensual fire,
i'm hidden as the sheep, cloaked in wolf's attire,
hiding the desires my soul secretly admires.
so why would she want me?
why?

lipstick on a toad

lipstick on a toad
a princess shouldn't be forced to accept
the pauper who knows nothing except
regret, sorrows of perpetual rain
a princess needs a sane prince to reign
for fame, of the Camelot her heart will raise
but i bring war, catapults that raze
insane, miseries of a lovely illusion
non-profit promises of poetic allusion
confusion is all my intentions elicit
when our love is a drug, smuggled and illicit
an explicit tryst for a princess isn't fair
she deserves much better, can't pay his own fare
compare the lover whose love leaves a hole
to a prince whose power makes her life whole
bold were those little handwritten presents
but words can't bless her with a palpable presence
lipstick on a toad

you and me

you and me
pancakes and bananas topped with strawberry cream aren't sweeter than your kisses, but oh, how i dream that earths would quake and tumble steel beams, crumble prison walls that lie in between . . . of . . .
you and me
delusions of your touches consume until i scream; phantoms of your lips crush mine to smithereens — have me praying for the day when our lusts will convene, and we lay up in the fantasies i have clearly seen . . . of . . .
you and me
please, let this infinite loneliness cease so i may rest my head on your cloud, a small peace; white cotton of the sky, bedded with silver sheets will be the texture of my breath when our bond is complete — the bond . . . of . . .
you and me

fifteen minutes

– for Faten

fifteen minutes
never thought
such a short time
could make me evaluate
life and love and what
it means to find happiness
in my friend

my eyes close tight
her sweet voice
makes me wish to ease
her pains
financial ... emotional ... sensual
i envision my hands on her hips
as she smiles when we kiss
and the salt of her tears
dries between our lips
home ... together
when we have both felt
alone ... forever

in one prison phone call
she makes me evaluate
happiness, friendship, a lifetime of love
in just
fifteen minutes

mr. maytag

mr. maytag
my love rests
hidden in her utility closet.
door closed, cavernous black, i wait
as she travels the globe
soiling her clothes.
rounds of sweat stain her dress
where colliding bodies caressed.
saliva-shaped lips on her bra
where he kissed.
his seed splotched the lace
that encased her pubis.
mascara on her sleeve, smeared
with wiped tears, after
he left her
frazzled, wrinkled, funky.
she hurries to the safety
of my cell, shoving dirty laundry
from her baggage down my throat
in a haste to erase
his stench.
wash, rinse, spin.
hot water dissolves smudges from within,
but cold preserves her delicates.
i know which will not abuse
because i cannot
use her in the way i am used.
dents in my sides from uneven loads,
or loads too heavy to bear, knocking
me against the wall.
no matter.
i handle this woman's work with
a man's strength, until
she leaves me, anew, wearing vibrant
reds, greens, and blues — and
with no trace of the stink

she once knew.
but she does leave.
i keep just one small thing:
a little lavender sock, whose
absence may make her stop
and return . . . looking.
just like before, again and
again, i will
wait to
wash, rinse, spin
when she comes back
frazzled, wrinkled, funky,
and sullen.
mr. maytag

i, sorrow

i, sorrow
whispers in the dark, phone beneath a cloth.
locked in the cage where my manhood was wrought.
confessing true love, as if i had ever known it,
yet realizing i've lost love wherever i have shown it.

and then, she mutters . . . "if."

"if . . . only i wasn't here, or . . .
if . . . you weren't in there . . ."

so i think,
if . . . clouds were cotton candy, storms might color our hair.
if . . . our hearts had never been broken, they'd need no
    repair.
if . . . i was by her side, she'd feel no despair.
if . . . only i wasn't here . . . or . . . if . . . she wasn't out there!
i've dealt with more ifs than ten hearts could compare!

i swear, years are tears spewing from thine eyes.
think i blinked twice and two fucking decades passed by.

but even that's not sorrow, not the sorrow i know.
sorrow is falling for love with no parachute or rope.
sorrow is raging rapids in a boat that won't float.
sorrow is letting go . . . for her happy tomorrow.
i, sorrow

ceaseless change

ceaseless change
winds change, as do hearts
storms won't end, violent as they start
oceans and seas must someday dry
into salt, as tears from our eyes
ceaseless change

the inheritance

the inheritance
my father told me a story once
it was only one of a few . . . you see
he was a stranger
a deadbeat i barely knew . . . anyway
he ran me out the front door
into a ghetto summer outside
his little duplex was a waste of space
on chicago's black southside
he pointed up forest avenue
like a man waving a gun
squinting at some invisible foe
escaping on the run
"your grandpa stood right here," he said
"in a wife beater stained with paint
he shouted to that midnight burglar
'i may be drunk, but i sho' shoot straight'"
he laughed and slapped my back
he doubled over to wheeze
then he stood up clutching his belly
reminiscing his fond memory
the ghetto sun faded
to a dark, blackish hue
my grandpa died a dirty drunk
and so will the father i barely knew
the inheritance

Phillip's father, Phillip Smith I, in the mid-1970s in Chicago

Lesson 3: Hurt & Tragedy

just over the fence

just over the fence
through razor wire i watch cars drive by
on sundays i assume the cadillacs are driving to church
on mondays i guess the trucks are traveling to work
occasionally someone honks or waves hi
some just stare with a contemptuous eye
you can tell who's rich by the collars of their shirts
you can tell who's in love by the way women flirt
i've learned a lot about people, watching their cars drive by
why, sometimes i watch with nothing else to do
wishing i was in a car driving past too
just over the fence

life is death

life is death
courts differentiate between life and death
both will live oppressed until our dying breath
because
life
is
death
whether in red jumpsuits or brown pants we dress
we inhabit prison cells until no life is left
because
life
is
death
we think passing days promote hopefulness
hope is a farce overshadowing hopelessness
because
life
is
death
no one will press a needle in my flesh
yet life without parole is no more or less, because
life is death

Note: In North Carolina prisons, custody levels are color-coded. Death Row prisoners wear red jumpsuits, and Regular Population prisoners (including lifers) housed in medium and/or maximum custody facilities must wear brown pants.

suicide prevention

suicide prevention
like a leash cuffing the neck of
a dog,
or a dam holding back flood from
a bog.

like a heart froze cold from long
lost love,
or a cage designed to enslave
white doves.

like eyelids clenched to restrain
hot tears,
or mumbling nonsense to forget
lost years.

like fingers in a fist to keep
them strong,
i beg my resolve to please
hold on.
suicide prevention

children of the chain

children of the chain
during saturday cartoons in a polk youth center dayroom,
billy got his wig split with a broken-off broom.

other inmates laughed and ran off to spread the news
while billy lay dead, on the floor, until noon.

too old to be tamed, yet too young to be ashamed,
too stubborn for change, we were just children in chains.

rappers on the radio sung us the wisdom of life.
we learned of sex from pictures, masturbation at night.

films gave us role models with a gangster's insight.
scarface was our hero when toting pride to a fight.

too old to be reclaimed, yet too young to be insane,
too naïve to be blamed, we were just children in chains.

my celly was my brother; his pride, justification.
through his eyes i decide my actions are his contemplation.

from his failure i gained a bastardized education
of aging in prison where survival is graduation.

too old to be saved, yet too young to be enslaved,
too unknown to be named, we were just
children of the chain

the satirical comedy of life

the satirical comedy of life
a lifer entering prison quickly learns to see without seeing and to hear without hearing to preserve the convict code of secrecy, but this targeted ignorance also helps one cope with the anarchy embedded within the carceral culture. as the carousel of madness spins round and round ever faster, fools hop on it instead of trying to jump off, because this is prison, and this is how prison should be.

i know, but i do not know.

i awaken as muffled arguing invades sleep. through my upstairs cell window, i view two men going to blows while the night shift officer dozes behind his desk only feet away. my stretchy yawn echoes in the concrete cell. it is five-forty-three a.m., almost shift change. i shave with an electric razor to start my day.

i see, but i do not see.

chow call. soggy imitation eggs; chewy turkey sausage with gristle bits popping off molars like buckshot; milk, thick as curds and whey; watery grits float clumped icebergs tall as himalayas. two thugs sit and complain that rudy poot is a snitch. i eat. i leave.

i hear, but i do not hear.

in the block, rudy poot leans lazily against the c/o's desk, obsessively brushing his wavy hair, his molasses skin and gold tooth gleaming. he confesses to ms. no-name, the c/o now on post, "baby girl, when you walk, it look like two turkeys wrestlin' in yo' pants. goddamn." she giggles, maybe happy to pass the morning of a long, boring day. rudy poot smiles wider. "looka here," he says, "lemme send you some money to get your hair braided . . ." i head to the stairs. on the way, i pass the shower, where peanut hunches naked with the curtain open, masturbating while staring at ms. no-name, looking like a shaved albino baboon on meth with his fangs bared in intense concentration. i run past to the stairs.

i see, but i do not see.

byrd accosts me as i walk past his cell in a hurry. he smiles while hoisting a large painting. "what do you think of this one, luck?" i squint one eye, then ask, "why is your cocker spaniel wearing a mop?" byrd's smile frowns as he lowers the painting. "it's a lion, muh-fucka." i shrug. "eh . . . looks more like a cockeyed hyena to me." byrd jabs a finger at me as i turn toward my cell. "that's alright! yo' ol' hatin' ass! i'm gonna dedicate my first million to you, luck — you big-toothed muh-fucka!"

i hear, but i do not hear.

in my cell . . . peace. people present frustration, even when they don't mean to. personalities are lies in archetypal costumes borrowed from images adopted by a flawed society departed from idolizing individuality and truth in favor of materialism and combative discourse. so, i find solace in solitude. i sit. my black pen glides across white paper like an ice skater twirling for pleasure. my words dance no practiced choreograph. i allow kaleidoscopic images to spew from the volcano of my imagination and coagulate into molten tributaries that harden between spaced lines to form one solid idea: who needs people when paper and pen procure peaceful possibilities? but then, the loudspeaker blares, "phillip smith! report to visitation!"

i think, but i do not think.

in visitation, i grab the camera out of the cabinet and call families to a mural for a picture. when i get to b's table, his chubby but cute sister — who visits every week — bats her eyelashes. "hey, luck," she sings. "b gets out next month. do you think i could start visiting you?" her fingers caress mine resting on the table. i pull my hand back slowly. "probably not.

ready for your picture?" when she puckers a kiss on my way out, i pretend to miss it, because living like a monk is better than falling victim to emotions like lust, passion, and love when lifers are destined to die in prison. it doesn't matter if i want love; i can only survive without it.

i feel, but i do not feel.

chow call. an extraterrestrial, gray alien meat patty pocked with purple craters; frigid broccoli stalks masquerading as headless horsemen; two slices of white bread harder than the soles of caligula's sandals. i eat three sporkfuls of broccoli stalks. on the way out, three men argue over my uneaten scraps. i put the tray on the table and leave. just outside, two burly c/o's lead jj, the prison dope dealer, to the hole in handcuffs. a convict walking near me mutters, "i told that fool not to trust rudy poot. now look at 'im. probably be on long-term lock up for a year." i keep moving.

i hear, but i do not hear.

back in the block. yard call. sunshine, no clouds. few men outside. seventeen pushups each minute for sixty minutes makes one-thousand-twenty. this is the only time throughout the day that i watch the clock. the passage of time brings me one minute closer to death in prison. i usually do not want to know the time. a hard-earned sweat expels salt and accumulated stress. on my way to the shower, i spot a-rod twanking out on synthetic marijuana. the drug, K2, is so potent that he is stuck like a statuesque zombie fighting drug-induced paralysis in short bursts resembling a seizure. i head to my cell thinking, why would anyone want to smoke that shit?

i see, but i do not see.

count time. quiet descends over the block in a fog as noisemakers are locked in cells to be tallied like tarnished pennies in a jar. i try to pick up my earlier project, but the scattering of random words read as gibberish. i put down the pen, lean back in my chair, and i close my eyes. the usual echoing chaos of a prison cellblock is a memory. i hear my heart beating. the gentle th-thump, th-thump, th-thump makes me relish life, even locked in a cage. the count clears, releasing cons like stampeding cattle as cell doors pop open. i step onto the mezzanine and lean on the rail, looking down. two men rush rudy poot when he exits his cell. sharp objects glint. sneakers squeak on the concrete floor, screeching loud as wounded animals. as rudy poot tries to fight back, harsh breathing fills my ears. i realize it is my own ragged breath. a wet, meaty schtick jerks hot blood in a spray each time they yank the shanks out, turning rudy poot's gray shirt red.

i wish i could see, but not see.

a dozen officers run in shouting, "lock down!" i move toward my cell, but i continue watching the men stab rudy poot. the c/o's eject retractable batons and attack them all, employing violence to combat violence. i go in my cell, sit down, and i listen. the beating stops. handcuffs clasp. walkie-talkies stop squawking. and i write, forcing myself to see, hear, know, think, and feel my imagination because my reality is too real to process without it . . .

>   poem within a poem
>   violets sprout from black soil
>   warm lips kiss cold of the dead
>   violence begets the blood we toil
>   but beauty blooms in silence
>   poem within a poem

i forget, but i do not forget.

the lockdown lasts all day. chow call. bagged lunches with shrink-wrapped baloney chewy enough to blow bubbles; cheese slices elastic as fruit roll-ups; apple juice saltier than piss in the dead sea. i sit alone thinking about my day and the lessons i learned.

> who needs people when paper and pen procure peaceful possibilities?

solace lies in solitude.
people present frustration, even when they don't mean to.
so, i leave people alone.

at nine-thirteen p.m., fifty c/o's in camouflage storm the block to ransack cells for weapons. i am strip-searched, then forced to walk in boxers through the block to step around a metal detector to see if i am hiding a knife up my rectum, while female c/o's appraise my nudity like a slave on the auction block. two c/o's toss my cell worse than a hurricane through florida. it takes an hour to wipe boot prints from my mother's photo after they leave my home for the next down the tier. strangely, they only confiscate one yellow highlighter, leaving two. go figure. they exit the block at two-twenty-seven a.m. the lights go out. finally. i realize that i watched the clock more in this one day than i have in twenty-one years because i could not wait for it to be over. i lay down for sleep thinking, damn, it's only tuesday.
the satirical comedy of life

gunslinger

gunslinger
he stood in the o-dorm hall
leaning against a wall, with
his hand shoved past the hole
cut in his pocket.
his fist pumped,
making it look like a murder
of crows
pecked at breadcrumbs
in his crotch
as he focused on officer
no-name calling out mail to
dozens gathered around her.

the gunslinger,
gunning her down.
no shame?
no remorse.

what drove him? her skin,
smooth as a chocolate bar? or,
tight pants with a booty that stars
spend fortunes to duplicate? or,
was it his own perversion?

she saw.
rolled her eyes.
"brownsville, get yo'
nastymuthafuckinassawayfrommebefore
i
lock
you
up!"

he fled not. strokes
quickened, fueled by rejection as

they engaged in a
cold war. she,
authoritarian. he,
rebel, determined to win this
one battle as recompense for all
those he'd lost. he could not
strike her, lest he be beaten. he
could not kill her, lest he be
killed. yet, this
one thing he could do
to exert his power, his rage, his
hurt, his sadness, his isolation, his
victimization, and his pain from incarceration.

officer no-name saw
that he would not stop.
she huffed,
then went back to mail call.

he convulsed in climax, then
walked to the bathroom to
wash away his victory.

i had witnessed rape
at high noon, because
he'd forced himself
upon her, even though
her protest equalled,
"*NO!*"

no convict approached him.
no convict reproached him.
we gritted teeth, balled fists, hated him
for his act, and ourselves for
not stopping it. to mastur-rape was
not accepted but tolerated as a
regularity in prison.

in secret, i complained to an
old coon who took me

to school. "nigga kill you over
one 'dem girls, youngblood. sho' as shit.
even if he only
jackin'. see,
in his messed up mind, that's his
old lady, and they's havin'
a conjugal
visit."

the gunslinger.
gunning her down.
no shame?
no remorse.

me? i had self-control. i ordered
semi-nude pictures of porn
stars dressed in lingerie, simulating
sex, from predatory companies that
existed only to satisfy desires
of the incarcerated.
what i did
was normal.

when i covered my cell window with
paper to thwart onlookers,
i set out on a honeymoon to
consummate marriage with whichever
picture landed on top. it was
release from the
noise, the fights, the oppression, and
it was
private.
i was

the gunslinger.
gunning her down.
no shame?
no remorse.

no conjugals here. we get
one embrace and one kiss at
the beginning and end of a
sterile, two-hour visit.

they banned nude images in '01, citing
rehab for sex offenders and
anger from female employees
searching our property.

they thought they were
doing god's work by
forcing felons to become
monks, devoid of
desire, devoid of
passion, devoid of
sexual normalcy, devoid of
our innate human nature.

as if we could forget
the sensuality of sugar summoned by
memory of its taste, simply
because they withheld it
for decades.

absence cannot construct abstinence

for when loneliness shivers my
bones worse than chattering
cold, i would trade my life to
touch, to kiss, to love, and
i sometimes covet sex and
companionship more than i covet
freedom.

as a result of systemic
ignorance and miscalculations of
ass-backward
decisions,
they created

the gunslinger.
gunning her down.
no shame?
no remorse.

the problem
was so prevalent that they
passed a law years back
allowing a gunslinger's
prosecution in
criminal court.

around the same time, they
allowed transgender people to
purchase panties, lipstick, bras,
makeup, and tampons from
the commissary in
all-male prisons. what were they
trying to do to heterosexuals?

so quick to punish for
hurt
we caused, but no recognition
of the
hurt
caused us.

and one time . . .

college students surveyed us at
central prison. a young white
woman fidgeted while asking if
i felt guilty after
masturbation.
when i finished laughing
in her face, i said,

"i'm twenty-four with life.
i will die in prison."
the only pleasure
i know
is as a
gunslinger

ode to oroonoko

ode to oroonoko
they sailed us over the ocean on slave ships
bound our wrists with chains and gagged our lips

    the prison busy stretched wide as a boat's gullet
    i stared out at freedom lost, my mood and thoughts
    sullen

they fed us stale rice and salty water
stole us to a new land where our old souls were bartered

    they locked me in a cage, but named it a cell
    condemned me to prison, but i knew it as hell

one day, warrior... next day, slave
i'll be hearing war drums until the silence of my grave

    a c/o asked my name. i told him jamoan.
    he pointed to my ID. "your name is 0273621."

that oroonoko the prince, in his general's sash
won our last battle, then sold me to the lash

    and then i saw him here, sopping gruel at chow
    hiding his face, keeping his head down

i wondered how oroonoko himself won chains
to america picking cotton, far from african plains

    he never ventured to the yard, lest he be found out
    last time i saw him, he was raiding my house

if ever there was a fool whom i'd wish to not know his name
it would be oroonoko, enslaver, now enslaved

    as my son lay a-slumber, alone in his bed

        police broke in to arrest me, but shot my child
           instead

'twas bittersweet justice to see him toiling beside
bleeding at the fingers with those he'd stripped of pride

        we nicknamed him caesar as a mock to his station
        once prince of purgatory, now damned to
           incarceration

starving in the night, while lusting for the feasts
when he supped with the king, foes kneeling at his feet

        with the protests on tv, crowds chanting, "BLM!"
        we backed caesar into a corner, then protested
           against him

in the dark of night, he escaped the plantation
fleeing the bondage of a white, christian nation

        they caught him in the woods, not far from the
           prison
        only a warrior could have survived the beating he
           was given

alas . . . my tribe once revered him as evil
but he was just a broken man who subjugated his people

        i saw him again, revenge still strong in my heart
        yet i wept in my cell, watching our captors tear him
           apart

i met his eyes, as he raised a weakened hand
in a strained voice he called, "brother! now i understand!"
ode to oroonoko

Note: This poem is loosely based on Aphra Behn's 1688 novel
Oroonoko: or, the Royal Slave, a tale about an African prince

who once sold prisoners of war as slaves to Europeans before being tricked into slavery himself.

an insufficient apology

an insufficient apology
when i was a kid, getting into
kid trouble, i cried and apologized
when caught. older, the troubles
grew bolder, yet i cried and said
i'm sorry.
my mom used to say, "son, there
will come a day when 'sorry'
isn't good
enough."

i wish she had been wrong.

while awaiting trial, i fired my
first attorney. eight months passed
since my arrest, and he had not given
me the evidence the state planned to
use against me. he was one of two
black lawyers in raleigh. inmates in my
cellblock said he smoked crack. would get
dope on credit and disappear for a year
without paying. he did not answer my
calls. i couldn't put my life in a man's
hands who wouldn't pick up the phone.

my second court-appointed
lawyer was white. not better.
actually worse. far worse. but
he got me a copy of the state's
evidence his second day on the
job. for that, he was okay.

the housing dorms of wake county
jail were no more than color-coded
concrete cages. men argued, laughed,
rapped, cursed, prayed, fought, and

farted all day long, because we
had nothing else to do. night —
when the rambunctious recharged —
i found peace to read.

within the quiet confines of my
cell, i sat on my steel sink with
the state's evidence balanced on
my lap. the sink was positioned beneath
the night light, illuminating the five-
hundred page stack of loose leaf
paper with letters; words; sentences;
paragraphs; in its dull indigo glow.

i read, hoping to understand why the
district attorney offered no plea and would
go straight to trial for life. i hoped to
find some loophole that may turn the
tides, like a home run in the ninth inning,
sailing over the wall. after all,

i had a gun; you had a gun.
why wasn't that fact
important?

i found no loophole.

i read how your daughter entered
this world
only days before
you left it.
were you at her birth? did you
welcome her trembling, screaming, and
afraid? did you have the chance to
comfort and calm her, as
your father consoled you? if only for
that moment? first and last
together?

the totality of such a loss
dawned on me . . . later . . . when
i met my nephew during
a prison visit at central prison,
where visitation was a prison
cell with a wall between my prison
hell and the world beyond. a barred
window — about the size of a small
tv — gave me a glimpse of a little
brown boy, swaddled in blue.

how i yearned to hold that child. to
tickle, teach, and train him to be a
better man than me. yet the wall kept
us apart, as a barrier between, and my
warm fingertips caressed only cold concrete.

for you and your daughter, the barrier
cannot be breached by voice, by sight,
nor by letter. i watched my nephew
grow
in loud visitation halls from a boy to a
man, but i did watch him
grow.

i hated myself for living
life, when you could not.
i hated myself much more
than before
the reading.
not only had i destroyed
our lives, but her life
too
because she would never know you.

i kept reading . . .

statements from your family and
friends told me all i needed
to feel worse.

you were someone's
son, brother
friend, lover
gone too soon.
long before
the world
truly knew
you.

as i read,
an apparition materialized
out of air. ethereal like a
hologram, but there.
twenty-something, handsome,
talented . . .

the state's evidence told me that
you had serenaded your high school in
a quartet. sang like an angel, yet . . .
you became homeless, couch surfing,
wandering the world
for a stage, like an
artist in search of the perfect
easel to paint your
masterpiece.

i lowered the documents to look at
your ghostly presence,
flickering like a lamp losing
its light.
you seemed so real that i could
touch your face. i saw you, and i
saw myself within you.

a black boy lost in a
world that would rather see him
shot or locked
up than heading a board meeting or
the white house. too bad we were

too young to know it. blinded by
modernity and a thinly veiled
farce of equality. too bad we
were too blind to see.

i remember . . .
well the night we met
in winter.
i had been released from prison
two, three weeks before. was forced
to wear my friends' clothes, because
i had none of my own. i zipped up
his leather jacket to ward off the
chill. who knew it would get much
colder?

your friends were strangers, as mine
were to you. your friends on break from
college. mine on break from prison.
bonded by weed and cheap booze.

you and i,
introduced by coke.
one a dealer, one a druggie.
who was which?
perhaps each a little of both.
it doesn't matter now, because
less than a month later,
both our lives ended
together.

in a statement, someone wrote
that you became homeless after arguing
with your roommates. and, that
you were trying to get your life
together for your newborn.

many can't understand how
a man could sell drugs and destroy
lives in order to save just one.

the same people can't understand
why a moth flies to the flame, searching
for freedom but finds death. they consider
both foolish. like the moth, we
could not know how our actions
would lead us too close to a hot
flame — too close to retreat. for
we all think of an escape
before realizing
there is none after we catch
fire.

i understood.
i understand.

love for your daughter
put you in the car that night,
as you chased a leg up
on life.

i understood.
i understand.

my first night out of
prison, i had to beg a friend to
sleep on the floor in his mother's
home. after all the promises i'd
made to be better after getting
out. i had no money, no clothes, no
plans. no hope. desire for a better
life was knocked off course by
reality: criminal record, black skin,
poverty. better? when someone offered
me weed to sell, i thanked god for
providing manna. i sold drugs — not to
feed a daughter, but — to feed
myself.

you understood.
you understand.

when i grew tired of the reading, i put
down the pages, but i kept seeing . . .

the inside of a dark car. two guns
pointed. two sinners and martyrs
anointed.

sweating. talking faster than ever.
trying to escape something i should have never
done.
the collision of our collective bad
choices amounted to one sum. an exploding
gun.

tears ran like rivers
in disguise. made me sink
to my knees before your
ghostly
eyes.

in my jail cell, i saw you
holding your daughter. i whispered,
"i am so sorry. i didn't know your
gun was plastic. i didn't know
you couldn't hurt me. i'm sorry i
took you from your family. i'm
sorry that i took your
life."

when i awoke, curled on the cold
concrete floor, the state's evidence lay
scattered about like confetti. i heard
my mother's voice. "son, there
will come a day when sorry
isn't good
enough."

yet i still offer
an insufficient apology

mammaw

mammaw
after grandad grunted off to work,
mammaw helped me tug on my
winter coat. we left the house
just as her god finger-painted the
watermelon sky with golden streaks
of sweet mango.

i skipped beside, refusing to hold
hands, pretending to be grown. her
sawed-off broomstick clopped out of
rhythm like a lame third foot against the
slushy brine sidewalk. the stick, not for
walking, meant to fend off chicago
goons trying to rob us, or worse.

this morning's walk carried us past cedar
park cemetery — an endless property enclosed
by a tall concrete wall. exotic shrieks
vaulted over that wall, conjuring images
of armored warriors chopping swords
toward ferocious pterodactyls striking
back with razor-sharp talons
of death.

i snatched mammaw's hand
as we passed. "boy, what are you
doing?" she asked. i stared terrified
up into her dark eyes and wrinkled
butterscotch face. "you don't even
know what you're afraid of," she added.

"a m-m-m-monster," i whispered, shivering.

mammaw gripped my hand tight and
dragged me across the street to the

wall. the toes of my british knights
clipped the curb as she jerked me
over it.

we walked to a split where two sections
of the wall joined unevenly. the settling
foundation had pulled them slightly
apart. "look," she said,
shoving me.

i dared not disobey. my hindparts
still wore the handprints
of her fury.

my palms shook as i pressed them
to the frigid wall. i closed one eye
and squinted through the crack.

inside, headstones stood in frozen
ranks like toy soldiers left outside on
a tabletop battlefield with snow
bulging as helmets. again, a shriek
cut the air. mammaw's firm hand
held me in place. "look, boy."

between two headstones, a dark
animal with a slender neck bopped
into the open with a long, colorful
tail dragging a canyon in the snow.
suddenly, the tail lifted and spread,
blooming into a greenish-blue plume
with iridescent, eyelike spots
traveling up the feathers. this time,
when it cawed, i laughed.
"it's just a
bird, mammaw.
it's just a pretty
bird."

"they only let them out for

a little while if it snows, so they
can stretch their legs," she said.
then, mammaw leaned down and
whispered, "sometimes . . .
the thing you fear most
is the thing you should confront.
it might not turn out to be so bad."
mammaw

Phillip's maternal grandmother, Lessie Finley, around 1978

Lesson 4: Injustice

no coal burning

no coal burning
an old coon, black as boot strap molasses,
told me of a past rite
in prison when
black and white
could not unite.

they called this practice
no coal burning.

as a child in
the american nation,
i did not grow up in
legal segregation.
of course i struggled with
racial separation, though we were
a century from emancipation.

as a boy in preschool,
i kissed a white girl.
the teacher jerked us apart
to preserve our
separate worlds.
"you can't do that!"
her hurled words slurred.
in the car ride home,
i told mama about my sin.
i begged to be white
so maybe i could kiss
my friend.

black boys teased me
for talkin' proper.
they jumped me in junior high
for hanging with white rockers.
they renamed me oreo,

called my friends wiggers.
they made me hate myself
for not acting like
a nigger.

four hundred years
we fought to be free.
cops killing us in the streets
but they ridiculed me.
like a cross in the dark,
its orange flames churning.
i felt boxed in by the rule
of no coal burning.

i let it dictate my actions
for years to come.
i toned down my intelligence,
made my vocabulary dumb.
i lost the potential of
who i could truly be
by relinquishing the purity
of my identity.

i blamed my critics
for making me turn,
when it was my own insecurity
that wouldn't let my coal burn.

like a match to a black clump
for a flame's yearning,
we lose ourselves by
instituting the rite of
no coal burning

appropriate violence

appropriate violence
today, i read a judgment from the bench
toward a teen who shot little kids without a flinch.
the judge tipped his glasses, then pointed a finger
to say, "i hope those inmates put you through the wringer."
now, if i had been present, which i was not,
i might have taken the floor and forced the judge to stop,
saying, "pardon me, i have some questions, if i may?
why is violence appropriate only when you say?
or, how can you give someone five hundred years
in hopes his blood will somehow cleanse tears?
as if judgment and violence share a comradery
and this notion of justice proves no hypocrisy,
sending people to prison supposedly for correction
then reveling when they avenge, for you, in dereliction.
is this the intention of our judicial section,
to employ incarceration as a diabolical weapon?
injustice created a system with no feeling.
since it doesn't work, why not try healing?
because if physical pain is an appropriate remedy,
you might as well give every felon the death penalty."
appropriate violence

raising cain

raising cain
my christian ethics professor
quoted exodus 20:13; specifically,
the sixth commandment, reading:
"thou shall not murder" as
justification for the death penalty
to a class full of killers serving
life without parole.

i thought
is he saying i deserve to die?

"the LAW of exodus 21:24," he
bellowed, "declares an eye for an
eye. tooth for tooth.
(and dramatically)
a DEATH ... for a ... DEATH!"

in the shallows of
tactical interpretation,
even a recipe for oatmeal cookies
shouted in german may sound like
hitler addressing a mass of nazis
to someone who
only speaks swahili.

in the shallows of
interpretation manipulation
politics stains scripture
like dye in clear liquid
to whatever color they choose
to tint
the glasses of those too ignorant
to see how once
muddied, water can never
regain purity. it remains

forever fouled.

but ... for those who
wade
in the deeper waters of
context,
the truth is as beautiful as
a dolphin
sailing through the
sky. you see ...

when cain slew abel,
his god did not follow the
law of a death for a death.

he banished cain for
seven years.
not 147 to 289 months
not twenty-five to life
not LWOP
not death
SEVEN ... years
to wander the wild
under divine protection.
not condemnation.

beneath the soot-black skies
cain heard abel's cries
each time he closed his eyes

his fists curled into mallets
like the hammers he
beat his brother with, but
this time, the clenched fists
were the result of his own
pain. internal, yet somehow
the same.

sequestration trapped him like
a man trapped in a cell

devoid of connection, love,
brotherhood, and
hope.

a slide show of horror
flicking across his memory like
shadow puppets backlit by
a dying candle.

he remembered abel's face
frozen in pain — pain
caused by cain's hand.

a brother slain by
a brother.

within his finite isolation,
cain realized that
there was nothing worse
than feeling
lonely.

and he wished his brother's
blood, calling from the grave,
was actually abel in the flesh
rejoicing in his name.

after his sabbatical,
cain settled and built the
city of nod. what
learned christians consider
the first civilization.

he raised a family who
pioneered farming and
invented tools, and whose
blood may run through the veins of
us all.

why did cain's god use he

who committed an uncivilized
act to teach humanity
what it means
to be civilized? perhaps ... because

those who have experienced
death truly understand the
value of life. for without
pain, we cannot desire the
healing. and without pain, we
cannot teach others to
avoid it.

who better to lead
the wicked
to redemption
than one who
survived damnation?

jesus knew.
he taught against the
exodus law of an eye
for an eye in matthew 5:38.

as i sat listening to
my christian ethics professor,
i wished he had read
that verse instead.
raising cain

banned books

banned books
worldly parents argue over
what to teach
the bluest eye ... or ...
james and the giant peach

with no regard for how
politics erases heritage
like ... prejudiced statues
face down in hedges

you want kids to learn
the greatness of your concerns
while all we discerned
should be erased ... or burned

i know censorship
it crippled me blind
and if i could ever see
knowledge proved hard to find

in the carceral desert
where convicts barter
banned books like
bedouins for clean water ... because

they made the new jim crow illegal
as they tried to hide
how they trap colored people
deep inside

they promote urban novels
instead of nietzsche or plutarch
to keep us ignorant
and perpetuate the farce

that criminals are dumb
worthless, lazy fools
while withholding education
except for christian schools

to make sheep from shepherds
or lambs out of bulls
to turn leaders to followers
who fall for what they pull

but worldly parents argue
over what to teach
the bluest eye ... or ...
james and the giant peach
banned books

a moral dilemma

a moral dilemma
white public pretender.
white state prosecutor.

white jury led in.
who is foreperson?
pretty blonde, soft blue eyes?
or balding man, grimacing to scrutinize
this dark smudge
on his starched white shirt?
what difference does it make?
one must read the unanimous verdict.

charcoal black judge occupies
the bench. hair white as pillow
stuffing. slouching over papers,
glasses teeter on his nose.

white prosecutor spews legalese,
sounding foreign as taiwanese to
the ignorant. boredly, charcoal black
judge sighs, "i will allow it." white
public pretender says . . . (drum roll) . . .
nothing.

pecan defendant is nineteen.
on trial for conspiracy to commit
first-degree murder. facing life without
parole. no haircut for thirteen
months. malnourished, pipe cleaner
limbs swallowed by an oversized
pumpkin jumpsuit with someone else's
skidmarks browning the back. on the
table before him rests a dog-eared copy of
No End in Sight, an article published by
the sentencing project. he ain't no

scholar, but he memorized the numbers.
he wonders if charcoal black judge
knows how the u.s. incarcerates/enslaves
one-point-four million.
sixty-percent are poor/insignificant/black.
just like him.
surely, he must know.
he's black, too.
how could he not know?
and if he does . . .
does he give a damn?

pecan defendant imagines . . .

charcoal black judge at nineteen,
walking ghetto streets
far removed from the current zeitgeist
of trunk-rattling hip hop beats.
on one corner, he stops to hear
a quartet snapping in time, singing
doo-wop sweetly. police speed up.
they beat one of the singers.
charcoal black judge stands
helpless/mortified/traumatized
as his friend is hauled off to jail.
anger drove him to the law.
he took the bench to right
systemic wrongs he did not create,
but after an eternity of seeing
black faces, time after time,
committing crimes
his activism became cynicism.
he once played ball in the same parks.
his discernment became resentment.
he shopped with the same grocer, and no
matter how poor, never thought of
robbing it.
his mercy became fury.
his success did not make him discredit
their weakness, but it forced a desire

to help them see/understand/shun their
errors. how else to do that . . . than
to punish?

spare the rod, spoil the child.

and charcoal judge stopped looking
for a better way.

pecan defendant locks eyes with
charcoal black judge. hope lies
not in the exchange. so he closes
his eyes. in reverie, he sees a
brass balance, white powder in one
pan, black powder in the other. the
pans weigh evenly. pecan defendant
finally understands. the equality of
white and black had never been in
question.

the hand of the pourer wields the
power to force the scale of justice
tilting one way or the other.

when pretty blonde stands
with the verdict, her
soft blue eyes sharpen into
daggers of ice as she reads,
"we, the jury, find the defendant
GUILTY."

why doesn't it matter that pecan defendant's
cousin robbed the store and
shot the clerk while he slept
in the car? pecan defendant never knew
what happened until they took him to jail.

north carolina incarcerates/enslaves
four-thousand-one-hundred-seventy lifers.
pecan defendant no longer wonders if

charcoal judge knows the numbers.
pecan defendant is just one grain of
sand weighing down imbalanced
scales of justice.

as pecan defendant stands for sentencing,
he prepares to become lifer number
four-thousand-one-hundred-seventy-one.
a moral dilemma

a hopeless hustle

a hopeless hustle
i'm penitentiary rich,
and i ain't no snitch
i sell suboxone and K2 ...
sheeit, dispensaries in colorado
ain't got trees like i do.
i got accounts in florida,
a prepaid debit card in maine,
a cashapp in california,
but ain't none of 'em
in my name.

i did it all behind the wall
in the last thirty-seven years.
buildin' me an empire
one day
be bigger'n sears.

see ... at the age of twenty-three
a judge gave me life.
had me slavin' on a prison farm,
tired as fuck at night.
i earned less than three dollars a week
bustin' my ass with little food and no sleep.

yeah ... i learned quick
i ain't built for pickin' beans.
they had no way to hurt me
with no hope for release.

i ain't like those
nickel and dime tramps
who smear toothpaste on envelopes
so they can recycle stamps.

when i first came in,

i ain't have shit.
now i move more bags
than lays be movin' chips.

i got snow-white sneakers
in thirty different cells.
i collect exotic colognes
in a variety of smells.

broke niggas travel
in dusty-ass shoes.
breath smellin' like an outhouse
at the ass end of june.

because they submitted to prison,
they relinquished their pride.
have no notion of self-worth,
find no ambition to rise.
they're scared to make a hustle,
scared of going to the hole.
they cannot fathom capitalism ... or
how a lifer could become
the black jeff bezos.

yet they prey on the weak
like some honey bun thieves.
hoping all they need to make it
is top ramen and squeeze cheese.

one time, i saved enough
to hire me a lawyer.
she drew up a pulitzer brief,
addressed the court like diane sawyer.

the judge looked down and said,
boy ... you got some nerve.
you shot a po-lice dog ...
death in prison is what you deserve.

he shipped me back to jail,

thirty-thousand down the drain.
but sometimes i wonder . . . is the judge
or myself to blame?

sheeit, i went back to hustlin'
'cause makin' money ain't so bad.
flippin' dope gave me a power
that freedom never had.

i got a buddhist nun
smuggles rum beneath her tunic.
she supplies hustlers stationed
in every housing unit.

i got a c/o chick
thicker than onlyfans models.
she brings whey protein and fish oil
still in the bottle.

all i do is get money, read,
and work out.
i'm living my best life
in the carolina big house.

as a hustler, i know
i represent the most hated
among my poor peers, and
especially the administration.
they toss my cell,
but nothing is ever taken.
i always trump the system
because i am
what it created.

i'm bigger'n morgan freeman was
in shawshank.
i got the goods he had,
plus andy's money in the bank.

i got it all, dog, i swear . . .

i control the seasons.
i got the prison hustler's dream,
but . . . i ain't got my freedom.
a hopeless hustle

ho-ass nigga

ho-ass nigga
a youth has a habit of disrespect
by making snide comments under his breath

petite, but thinks he's built like a gorilla
boasting out loud: "I'm sick of these ho-ass niggas"

ho (hō) 1. a derogatory noun. 2. a euphemism for bitch
defining a coward reluctant to throw his fists

after decades locked up, i have survived many wars
like a soldier at normandy bleeding on enemy shores

i understand the desire to establish a rep
if people fear your name, wolves circle you less

but i learned as a youth to check my pride
by walking with a con who'd spent his life inside

he taught me survival by extending respect
he showed me how crafty men did not need violence

at that time, lifers my age were few
it seemed easier to accept his advice at twenty-two

but now . . . our cages overrun with children
idolizing rappers who lie to make millions

instead of respect, they perpetuate hate, and
cannot differentiate between real or fake

to them, real is stabbing to solve problems, or
beating one's chest and going to the hole often

these ignorant youths do not understand
i made the same mistakes before becoming a man

many black boys are raised by amazons
single-women warriors whose men are gone

alone at home, social media and tv
taught them that manhood meant disrespecting me

because i'm over forty, don't look like a thug
they think i haven't felt their longing to be tough

i share their trauma, i have ingested their pain
i too have injured others to transfer my shame

and for what? an expression of masculinity?
when we're crying for help and searching for identity?

man . . . a "ho-ass nigga" ain't nothin' but words
i've been in prison so long that shit no longer burns

if they really knew me, they'd get down on their knees
and pay homage to the old coon defeating their enemies

this "ho-ass nigga" is an accomplished writer
i co-authored a bill to secure release for lifers

i no longer value the violence of henchmen
because my true foe is the criminal justice system

and i do fight . . . albeit in another way
but i refuse to fight the people i fight for every day

does that make me soft? does that make me a ho?
i accept today's disrespect to fight for better tomorrows
ho-ass nigga

i remain

i remain
a man was released today
he served only four years
for beating his baby to death
after consuming too many beers

yet, i remain

in an old folks' home
a crazy fool killed eight
got convicted of second degree
from LWOP he escaped

yet, i remain

i haven't caused any trouble
for over five thousand days
you won't hear a squeak out of me
in the midst of a violent blaze

yet, i remain

i saw a man stabbed
in his throat and chest
his assailant can't be punished
he'll be released week after next

yet, i remain

they locked me in a cage
no drug treatment or education
but i found a way to thrive
and to elevate my station

yet, i remain

i became well-versed in law
earned all a's in school
am a journeyman in graphic design
and i give my peers the same tools

yet, i remain

i taught myself guitar
became a literary savant
if they desire signs of change
what more could they want? yet . . .
i remain

grandad

grandad
i squirm atop the concrete stoop
as he pulls up in the oldsmobile.
i bound into his embrace as the
door creaks open, loosing work scents
of motor oil, sweat, and dirt.
"wha'chu know good, buddy?" he asks.
"nuttin' much, grandaddy."
our call and response echoes year
after year in a repeated negro
spiritual as a euphemism for
"i love you" because manhood
refused such expressions of
weakness.

after mammaw's southern, chicago-style
dinner, we walk to the corner store.
he jiggles the loose change in his pocket
then gives me some so i can jiggle change
too. "a man always needs change to
jiggle," he tells me. "don't ever forget it."
we buy one pint of breyers vanilla ice cream,
two cans of ice cold pepsi, and
two hostess lemon pies.

there are times — now — when
the suicide monkey climbs my back
to gnaw at me worse than
any narcotic i ever used to escape
the eternal suffering called life, and
i lay down, close my eyes, then hear
wind chimes clanking behind his house,
big band trombones jazzing as he
tinkers with the olds, pennies jingling
in his pocket as he walks, a child's
laughter above the rustle of crinkling

hostess lemon pie wrappers, him asking,
"wha'cha know good, buddy?" and my
tear-choked response as i
think about dying in a cage.
"nuttin' much, grandaddy. nuttin' much at all."

no matter how much sugar is added to lemon,
it maintains its bite. my tongue summons the
bittersweet remnants of swallowed pies, reminding
me of when i knew happiness, and maybe will
again, as i squirm on the stoop, waiting for
a hug, laughter, love, and hope.
grandad

Phillip's maternal grandfather, John Finley, around 1980

Lesson 5: Redemption

at the well

at the well
i once lived
near a field of daffodils.
in the center of that field
was an old-fashioned well.
its body was built of
solid stone blocks.
it stood just stout enough
for a little boy to climb atop.

i dropped the bucket
then turned its rickety crank,
watching in wonder
as the hollow vessel sank.
reflected in the pool
of that well below,
in water as pristine as
young eyes would ever know,
were the bark and branches
of my family tree —
veins in the leaves of those
who'd drawn before me.

in the well . . . were
shattered backs and broken spirits.
pain so great . . . no
other heartache could get near it.
i saw slave ships drifting
on tears in those ripples,
and arthritic hands that
had never clutched a nickel.

i witnessed jubilation
after emancipation, yet
a century passed before
they could vote in this nation.

jim crow tried to suppress them,
instead they arose,
singing, "we shall overcome," as
they shut down major roads.
they were attacked by police
in their quest for equal schools,
singing, "we shall overcome,"
but "we shall NOT be moved."

this is the sight . . .
the sight i saw
as i stared into the well with
wide eyes and slack jaw.

i saw black leaders rise
only to be shot down.
yet mourners held hands, chanting,
"i'm black and i'm proud!"
but somewhere down the line,
our path went astray.
with no captains at the helm,
our mothership lost its way.

a war on drugs
became a war on us.
we stopped holding hands in the streets
because the streets made us tough.
it was no longer in fashion
to love one another.
instead of fighting for our rights,
we sold drugs to each other.

for all the blameless trayvon martins and
innocent emmett tills,
the weight of my misdeed makes
their legacies stand still.

the dream of mlk
and the fist of malcolm x
have become lyrics by lil wayne

and a chorus of disrespect.

you think you are singular,
you claim to be one,
yet WE represent the whole
of all damages done.
for every child that dies
for every mother on her knees
the resolve of our ancestors
has fled our communities.

i ain't no saint.
i have done the worst wrong.
because of my transgression,
i am haunted by freedom songs.
yet i sit here today
confessing that it's never too late
to transcend race
and truly make america great.

for in that well
floats a blend of honor and hate
drawing from the same spring
and origin as fate.
i drew a full bucket
by its rickety crank.
for a long time i gazed
into my reflected face.
then i cupped my hands, drenched
them wet, and i drank,
hoping the pain i suffer will
somehow give you strength
at the well

recollection

recollection
when a hawk soared over the plains
the cry of its call resembled a name

he was not a titan of world renown
not a king, yet he donned a crown

filled with wisdom, he held no degrees
just a worker in prison, who inspired so many

he was the picture of strength, a rock of fortitude
with soft words of kindness and a laughter that soothed

during my darkest days i went to him sighing
he comforted my pain, even when he was dying

my little troubles were nothing compared to his
yet he never spoke of his end, only of how to live

for here was a man who never complained
accepting hardship and happiness as one and the same

so when that hawk cried out over the plains
i thought of smittie james flying free of his chains
recollection

Note: Smittie James was my friend and mentor before he died from cancer in 2019.

hope

hope
flickering beacon   beyond   an opaque fog
savior descending   as   a fleshly demigod
faint thumping   after   cardiac arrest
passage cleared   newborn   takes first breath
hope

Learning Instructions For Everyone

Learning Instructions For Everyone
life is a hot tear burning your eye,
when razor wire slashes your perfect blue sky.
life is entering prison with no fuzz on your face,
then — as decades pass — watching your beard turn gray.
life is living without purpose for endless years,
each january wondering why the hell you're still here.
life is hearing the phrase "you must have faith,"
but their faith ends in a pine box prison grave.
life is depression through self-degradation,
knowing you're better than mistakes you keep making.
life is rising for work seven days a week
and still can't afford snacks from the canteen.
life is disrespect from the mouths of overseers
and echoing hate from the mouths of peers.
life tortures the weak, pains the forsaken,
the strong fight on by learning to embrace it.
life is a steel mind, a weather-resistant will,
the audacity to succeed in a man-made landfill.
life is finding a way to love yourself
despite the pain and anguish you caused everyone else.
life is learning to scale towering walls,
to influence the world without leaving here at all.
Learning Instructions For Everyone

time

time
i used to be a slave to the clock
constantly checking my watch
willing it faster to tick tock

anxious for friends to arrive
anxious to shorten long drives
anxious to end my wait in lines

prison taught me to avoid those hands
to disregard the hourglass sands
because time . . . is an invention of man

constraining the limitless
into finite increments
removing focus from priceless sentiments

restricting our liberty to just be
in the moment for whatever moments mean
and the opportunity to truly be free

so now i take time to watch the sky
making note of how clouds fly
allowing time to slowly pass by
time

the introvert

the introvert
he spends days without
talking.

hunched over in his cell
writing.

lost,
his mind drifts farther than
the ss minnow, yet he
does not want this island
found.

while they seek
comfort in lies burnishing them
majestic, he seeks
discomfort in truths rusting him
human.

they shout TRIUMPH like echoes
down a holler, then laugh at how
much better empty words sound
coming back.
his thoughts trickle through a
sieve of modesty, though his
trophy case is too full
to add more.

he spoke once,
while venturing to
the land of the lost in search of hot
water for coffee. a christian asked
him to lead a prayer. the whisper
of his words made
walls tremble.

he recounted an ancient chinese
proverb about a hermit who
never left his cave.
the townspeople, fed up with greedy
leaders, begged the hermit to be
their king. when he refused to exit
his cave, they smoked him out
with noxious fumes. but, rather
than lead them in anything,
he cast himself
into the sea,
drifting farther than
the ss minnow.

when they fished the hermit out,
his corpse wore a bloated
smile.

he asked,
"what did the hermit know that
everyone else did not?"

instead of waiting for
an answer,
he walked
back to his cell.
the introvert

"what could prison be?"

"what could prison be?"
she asks ... so i muse ...

it could be fairness
instead of partisan hate,
an oasis of learning
where the weak become great

or ... a fountain of hope
in its waters we dance
beneath an azure sky
exulting a second chance
as a
symbol of the peace
we all desire
symbol of a society
free people would admire

in this elysium
cells serve as chambers, where
the remorseful channel anger
to heal broken strangers
        thieves = tutors
        rapists = saviors
        killers = mentors
animals who fell here
become men who stand again

disagreements could be doctrinal, but
never final ... hope would abound amid
humanism, theology, sociology, all
intellectual onslaughts as a new dynamic

if only we had education,
minimum wage to survive,
drug treatment for addiction

as reasons to thrive, or maybe
overseers with compassion
instead of iron fists
pounding us harder
into a hellish abyss, because
the helping hand of hope
must descend from above
and we need to experience
the assistance of love

with tears in my eyes
across the visitation table
i repeat her question
but more as a question
to myself

i muse . . . before asking . . .
"what could prison be?"

About the Poet

Phillip Vance Smith, II, is the editor of *The Nash News*, the longest-running prison periodical in North Carolina, and the co-editor of *Compassion*, a newsletter by and for incarcerated individuals. He spearheaded the placement of both publications on JSTOR, a digital library accessible to the public. His writing has been published in *Logic(s)*, *The North Carolina Law Review*, *Prison Journalism Project*, *The Humanist*, *Walk In Those Shoes*, and elsewhere. He has appeared on the podcasts *Criminal* and *Prison POD*. He is the co-author of The Prison Resources Repurposing Act, a legislative proposal that aims to decrease prison violence and reduce recidivism by giving prisoners with life without parole sentences a second chance through stringent educational, behavioral, and vocational programming. Phillip is currently finishing his Associate of Arts degree and works as a visitation photographer at Nash Correctional Institution, where he is currently located. He has been serving life without parole in North Carolina since 2002. He can be reached at phillipvancesmith2@gmail.com. Read more of his writing at katbodrie.com/pvs2.

Scan the QR code below to hear a recording of Phillip reading a few poems in this collection:

About the Artists, Editors, & Designers

Kat Bodrie, Book Editor, is an editor and poet in Winston-Salem, North Carolina. Her editorial credits include *Inside: Voices from Death Row, Interface, Bone Orchard: Reflections on Life under Sentence of Death, Winston-Salem Monthly*, and *Concussion Discussions: Vol. 2*. Her poetry has appeared in *Poetry South, West Texas Literary Review, Rat's Ass Review*, and elsewhere. She is President of Winston-Salem Writers and Host City Coordinator for Poetry In Plain Sight. A recovering community college instructor and tutor, she works with prisoners on their creative writing and frequently collaborates with George T. Wilkerson, who lives on Death Row in North Carolina. Read more at katbodrie.com.

Casey Chiappetta, Cover Designer, is an American University alumna who received her Master of Science in Justice, Law, and Criminology in 2019 and her Bachelor of Arts in Sociology in 2017. She is the recipient of the outstanding scholarship award at both the undergraduate and graduate levels, the first person to receive both prestigious awards. Casey currently works with The Pew Charitable Trusts. At Pew, she conducts research and manages research grants focused on making the civil legal system more equitable, open, and efficient. Prior, she worked at the National Legal Aid and Defender Association, providing technical assistance to civil legal aid and leading research on online dispute resolution. Her work has been published in *Disability & Society, Family Court Review*, and *MIE Journal*, among others.

Benjamin Feder, Art Director, is an honors graduate of American University, holding Bachelor of Arts and Master of Arts degrees in Art History with a focus on Humanism and the Italian Renaissance. His experiences as both an artist and a student of art history are what initially compelled him to start a career in the art industry. Benjamin has worked in museums and galleries in both New York City and Washington, D.C., and is currently working at one of D.C.'s top art advisory firms. As an artist, Benjamin's favorite medium is clay, though he often includes mixed media into his sculptures.

Ginger Finigan, Chief Editorial Officer, is an undergraduate student and writer at American University where she is studying Political Science with an emphasis in prison reform.

Robert Johnson, Publisher, is a professor of Justice, Law, and Criminology at American University and publisher of BleakHouse Publishing, which he founded in 2006. A widely published author of fiction and nonfiction that deals with crime and punishment, Robert has extensive experience interacting with and researching death row populations. His best-known work of social science, *Death Work: A Study of the Modern Execution Process*, won the Outstanding Book Award of the Academy of Criminal Justice Sciences.

Norah Nasser, Chief Operating Officer, is a current undergraduate student at American University. She is pursuing a Bachelor of Arts in Justice and Law with a concentration in Criminology. Norah is extremely passionate about prison reform and other social justice issues.

Lewis Whitmire, Cover Designer, is a self-taught, award-eligible graphic designer and entrepreneur, formerly a guest of the state where he was Assistant Editor of *The Nash News*, North Carolina's leading prisoner-published news magazine. Lewis is from Western North Carolina and currently resides there where he runs an online e-commerce business and manages the logistics and shipping for OurJourney, a state-wide, reentry nonprofit dedicated to bridging the gap from prison to freedom by connecting individuals to resources in their communities.

Praise for *LIFE*

"Prison walls isolate citizens from the life inside, so we are spared thinking about the daily realities facing the incarcerated. Smith's marvelous poems provide rich and emotion-triggering insights about this hidden world, showing how humanity and inhumanity exist side by side in the society of captives. We are given a unique and often disturbing education about an institution — the prison — that the United States employs more than any other advanced Western society."

Francis T. Cullen
Past President, American Society of Criminology
Distinguished Research Professor Emeritus
2022 Stockholm Prize in Criminology
University of Cincinnati

"No words can do justice to the experience of incarceration — particularly life and death sentences — yet somehow, Smith's raw, devastating dispatches from one of the darkest corners of human existence manage to convey messages of hope for us all, in prison and out."

Shadd Maruna
President, American Society of Criminology
Professor of Criminology
Queen's University Belfast

"*LIFE* is a critically important window into the realities of incarcerated life, realities I've seen close-up in my past work as a correctional officer and today, as an ethnographic researcher. Smith's poems are altogether authentic, concerning, reflective, empowering, hideous, and beautiful. A deeply moving book."

TaLisa J. Carter
Assistant Professor
Department of Justice, Law & Criminology
American University

"This collection illustrates the power of creative writing to connect us across time and space to the most profound and elemental aspects of human experience. Smith took up poetry as a form of therapy, and *LIFE* is testament to the strength found in vulnerability. There is beauty and truth in every line."

Yvonne Jewkes
Professor of Criminology
University of Bath

"Phillip Smith's compelling collection reminds us that there is crime and there is punishment, and more than we want to know, there is the crime of punishment that has metastasized into our bloated prison system. We are honored to add this book to the BleakHouse collection."

Robert Johnson
Founding Editor & Publisher
BleakHouse Publishing

Review of *LIFE*

To me, a man in prison, because I have to essentially experience the same day repeat itself endlessly, what captivates me is seeing the all-too-familiar portrayed in fresh ways. As a writer and avid reader, I often notice that certain themes keep popping up [in prison literature], and rarely do they offer a fresh perspective. However, *LIFE*'s poems, which are hard-won observations, reflections, and life lessons, come to us filtered through an incarcerated man who's served more than twenty years on a sentence of life without possibility of parole. I say the poems are "hard won" because, even when engaging in themes common to the genre of prison literature, they give us the sense of flying debris that was plucked, midair, as it tumbled by outside during a hurricane. The poems work to focus on details amid an intense and chaotic emotional, social, and physical landscape that's sometimes deadly. Literally. Things we know well look different when viewed through a storm.

An important tool to help center one's focus is the collection's solid structure. First of all, the book is divided into five main sections with thematic headings that distill what's to come. Secondly, each poem employs a device called "inclusio," which places the poem's title at both beginning and end, as its first and last lines. Smith chose to make his titles clear and functional and, combined with the inclusio device, this works like the opening and closing paragraphs in expository essays. Because the specifics in between these book-ends will be foreign to many (despite the familiar themes), as it explores extremities of inner and outer violences, the poems could easily induce disorientation and confusion — but for the titles. The titles, then, serve as both handrail and reference point all at once: something to hang on to and guide, and something to orient the reader and make sense of the content.

Thirdly, to tie all the sections together, *LIFE* employs a meta-inclusio in that the book's first poem title is also its last, but with a twist. This suggests the titles are not meant to be seen as a single point on a circle (both beginning and end). Rather, they convey the idea that on this journey of life, though we may try to return to what we once knew, the end will not be the same experience because the journey in between has changed us. So, too, does *LIFE* change the reader by its end. Even for a fellow prisoner such as me, it made new what I *thought* was familiar territory.

George T. Wilkerson
Four-time PEN award–winner incarcerated on Death Row
Author of *Interface*

Other Titles from BleakHouse Publishing

Bone Orchard: Reflections on Life under Sentence of Death, George T. Wilkerson and Robert Johnson

Interface, George T. Wilkerson

Crass Casualties, Anthony G. Amsterdam

Behind These Fences, E.L.

Pagan, John Corley

Silent, We Sit, Emily Dalgo

Black Bone: Poems on Crime and Punishment, Race and Justice, Alexa Marie Kelly

An Elegy for Old Terrors, Zoé Orfanos

Up the River, Chandra Bozelko

Distant Thunder, Charles Huckelbury

Enclosures: Reflections from the Prison Cell and the Hospital Bed, Shirin Karimi

A Zoo Near You, Robert Johnson et al.

Origami Heart: Poems by a Woman Doing Life, Erin George

Tales from the Purple Penguin, Charles Huckelbury

Burnt Offerings, Robert Johnson

Printed in the USA
CPSIA information can be obtained
at www.ICGtesting.com
LVHW011402100124
768548LV00101B/5746

9 780996 116299